LAMENT OF WOMEN
& Other Rhythms

BY
DJUNA BARNES

FORGOTTEN POETS

Editor | Dick Whyte   Number 22 | 2024

DJUNA BARNES (1892-1982) was born on Storm King Mountain, near Cornwall-on-Hudson, in New York. Her grandmother Zadel Barnes was a writer, journalist, and Suffragette activist, and her father Wald Barnes was a musician and painter. After her mother left her father, the family moved to New York City in 1912. Barnes attended the Pratt Institute and the Art Students League of New York for a time, and worked as a journalist for the *Brooklyn Daily Eagle*, becoming well-known as a feature writer, interveiwer, and illustrator. She was involved with Alfred Stieglitz's 291 Gallery, and in 1915 moved to Greenwich Village, known for its burgeoning art scene and bohemian values. The same year Barnes met Guido Bruno, who featured many of her drawings and poems in the magazine *Bruno's Weekly*, and published her first collection, *The Book Of Repulsive Women* (1915). In 1921 she moved to Paris, and lived there for the next 10 years, publishing two novels, and a collection of plays, short-stories, and poetry under the title *A Book* (1923). Barnes returned to Greenwich Village in the late-1930s, and remained there until her death in 1982.

Publication credits: The complete *Book of Repulsive Women* (Bruno Chapbooks, Nov. 1915); with 'The Dreamer' (*Harper's Weekly*, 1911); 'Call of the Night' (Dec. 1911); 'Somewhere' (*The Lady's Realm*, Sep. 1911); 'Serenade' (*Cavalier Weekly*, May 1914); 'Solitude' (Nov. 1914); 'Harvest Time' (May 1915); 'This Much & More' (Sep. 1915); 'Birth' (June 1916); 'A Last Toast' (Sep. 1916); 'To A Bird' (Sep. 1919); 'The Yellow Jar' (*Munsey's Magazine*, Sep. 1916); 'Shadows' (Nov. 1916); 'Lament of Women' (*The Little Review*, Dec. 1918); 'Lines to a Lady' & 'Antique' (*Harper's Weekly*, Aug. 1918). 'Hush Before Love', 'Paradise' & 'Pastoral' (*The Dial*, April 1920), 'Song In Autumn', 'Lullaby', 'I'd Have You Think Of Me', 'The Flowering Corpse', & 'She Passed This Way' (*Vanity Fair*, March 1923); 'To One Feeling Differently' (*Playboy*, 1923); 'First Communion' & 'Finis', from *A Book* (1923); & 'Finale' (*The Little Review*, 1918).

Cover: Djuna Barnes – 'Dobrujda' (*Vanity Fair*, December 1916) & 'Russian Ballet' (*Bruno's Weekly*, April 1916). Inside: Barnes – 'Five Drawings' (*The Book of Repulsive Women*, 1915); 'Self-Portrait' (*Pearson's*, Nov. 1923); 'Six Portraits' (*A Book*, 1923); 'Poet & Flower' (*Bruno's Weekly*, 1916); 'A Villager' (*New York Morning Telegraph Sunday Magazine*, 1916); portrait of Barnes "by Terry" at the Greenwich Village Inn (*Bruno's Weekly*, 1915); etc.

FORGOTTEN PRESS
Aotearoa | New Zealand

ISBN: 978-1-991310-17-0 (paperback) • 978-1-991310-18-7 (hardback)
978-1-991310-19-4 (ebook)

DJUNA BARNES
LAMENT OF WOMEN & OTHER RHYTHMS

THE BOOK OF REPULSIVE WOMEN

8 rhythms & 5 drawings, originally published as
The Book of Repulsive Women (1915).

A BOOK OF POEMS & PORTRAITS

26 rhythms & 10 portraits, originally published in
A Book (1923) & assorted magazines (1915-23).

A SHORT STORY: FINALE

Short-story, originally published in
The Little Review (1918).

FORGOTTEN POETS

edited by **Dick Whyte**.

—❦—

Missing Meters! Lost Lyrics! Vanished Verses!

LEWIS ALEXANDER
PEARL ANDELSON
IRIS BARRY
GWENDOLYN BENNETT
ADELAIDE CRAPSEY
MARY CAROLYN DAVIES
HILDA DOOLITTLE
HILDEGARDE FLANNER
F.S. FLINT
JUN FUJITA
SADAKICHI HARTMANN
T.E. HULME
TAKEKO KUJO
AMY LOWELL
MINA LOY
YONE NOGUCHI
CHARLES REZNIKOFF
EDWARD STORER
MARIE TUDOR-GARLAND
AKIKO YOSHINO
AKIKO YANAGIWARA
& MANY MORE

FORGOTTENPOETS.COM

DJUNA BARNES

THE BOOK OF REPULSIVE WOMEN

8 Rhythms and 5 Drawings

EDITED BY GUIDO BRUNO IN HIS GARRET ON
WASHINGTON SQUARE, NEW YORK

November, 1915

TO MOTHER

Who was more or less like all
mothers, but she was mine, and
so—She excelled.

From Fifth Avenue Up

SOMEDAY beneath some hard
   Capricious star—
Spreading its light a little
Over far,
We'll know you for the woman
That you are.

For though one took you, hurled you
Out of space,
With your legs half strangled
In your lace,
You'd lip the world to madness
On your face.

We'd see your body in the grass
With cool pale eyes.
We'd strain to touch those lang'rous
Length of thighs;
And hear your short sharp modern
Babylonic cries.

It wouldn't go. We'd feel you
Coil in fear
Leaning across the fertile
Fields to leer
As you urged some bitter secret
Through the ear.

We see your arms grow humid
In the heat;
We see your damp chemise lie
Pulsing in the beat
Of the over-hearts left oozing
At your feet.

See you sagging down with bulging
Hair to sip,
The dappled damp from some vague
Under lip,
Your soft saliva, loosed
With orgy, drip.

Once we'd not have called this
Woman you—
When leaning above your mother's
Spleen you drew
Your mouth across her breast as
Trick musicians do.

Plunging grandly out to fall
Upon your face.
Naked—female—baby
In grimace,
With your belly bulging stately
Into space.

In General

WHAT altar cloth, what rag of worth
　　Unpriced?
What turn of card, what trick of game
Undiced?
And you we valued still a little
More than Christ.

From Third Avenue On

AND now she walks on out turned feet
    Beside the litter in the street
Or rolls beneath a dirty sheet
      Within the town.
She does not stir to doff her dress,
She does not kneel low to confess,
A little conscience, no distress
      And settles down.

Ah God! she settles down we say;
It means her powers slip away
It means she draws back day by day
        From good or bad.
And so she looks upon the floor
Or listens at an open door
Or lies her down, upturned to snore
        Both loud and sad.

Or sits beside the chinaware,
Sits mouthing meekly in a chair,
With over-curled, hard waving hair
        Above her eyes.
Or grins too vacant into space—
A vacant space is in her face—
Where nothing came to take the place
        Of high hard cries.

Or yet we hear her on the stairs
With some few elements of prayers,
Until she breaks it off and swears
     A loved bad word.
Somewhere beneath her hurried curse,
A corpse lies bounding in a hearse;
And friends and relatives disperse,
      And are not stirred.

Those living dead up in their rooms
Must note how partial are the tombs,
That take men back into their wombs
     While theirs must fast.
And those who have their blooms in jars
No longer stare into the stars,
Instead, they watch the dinky cars—
      And live aghast.

Seen From the "L"

So she stands—nude—stretching dully
  Two amber combs loll through her hair
A vague molested carpet pitches
Down the dusty length of stair.
She does not see, she does not care
    It's always there.

The frail mosaic on her window
Facing starkly toward the street
Is scribbled there by tipsy sparrows—
Etched there with their rocking feet.
Is fashioned too, by every beat
      Of shirt and sheet.

Still her clothing is less risky
Than her body in its prime,
They are chain-stitched and so is she
Chain-stitched to her soul for time.
Ravelling grandly into vice
Dropping crooked into rhyme.
Slipping through the stitch of virtue,
      Into crime.

Though her lips are vague as fancy
In her youth—
They bloom vivid and repulsive
As the truth.
Even vases in the making
      Are uncouth.

In Particular

WHAT loin-cloth, what rag of wrong
    Unpriced?
What turn of body, what of lust
Undiced?
So we've worshipped you a little
More than Christ.

Twilight of the Illicit

YOU, with your long blank udders
    And your calms,
Your spotted linen and your
Slack'ning arms.
With satiated fingers dragging
At your palms.

Your knees set far apart like
Heavy spheres;
With discs upon your eyes like
Husks of tears,
And great ghastly loops of gold
Snared in your ears.

Your dying hair hand-beaten
'Round your head.
Lips, long lengthened by wise words
Unsaid.
And in your living all grimaces
Of the dead.

One sees you sitting in the sun
Asleep;
With the sweeter gifts you had
And didn't keep,
One grieves that the altars of
Your vice lie deep.

You, the twilight powder of
A fire-wet dawn;
You, the massive mother of
Illicit spawn;
While the others shrink in virtue
You have borne.

We'll see you staring in the sun
A few more years,
With discs upon your eyes like
Husks of tears;
And great ghastly loops of gold
Snared in your ears.

To a Cabaret Dancer

A THOUSAND lights had smitten her
    Into this thing;
Life had taken her and given her
    One place to sing.

She came with laughter wide and calm;
    And splendid grace;
And looked between the lights and wine
    For one fine face.

And found life only passion wide
    'Twixt mouth and wine.
She ceased to search, and growing wise
    Became less fine.

Yet some wondrous thing within the mess
    Was held in check:—
Was missing as she groped and clung
    About his neck.

One master chord we couldn't sound
    For lost the keys,
Yet she hinted of it as she sang
    Between our knees.

We watched her come with subtle fire
    And learned feet,
Stumbling among the lustful drunk
    Yet somehow sweet.

We saw the crimson leave her cheeks
    Flame in her eyes;
For when a woman lives in awful haste
    A woman dies.

The jests that lit our hours by night
    And made them gay,
Soiled a sweet and ignorant soul
    And fouled its play.

Barriers and heart both broken—dust
    Beneath her feet.
You've passed her forty times and sneered
    Out in the street.

A thousand jibes had driven her
    To this at last;
Till the ruined crimson of her lips
    Grew vague and vast.

Until her songless soul admits
    Time comes to kill;
You pay her price and wonder why
    You need her still.

Suicide

CORPSE A

THEY brought her in, a shattered small
    Cocoon,
With a little bruised body like
A startled moon;
And all the subtle symphonies of her
A twilight rune.

CORPSE B

THEY gave her hurried shoves this way
    And that.
Her body shock-abbreviated
As a city cat.
She lay out listlessly like some small mug
Of beer gone flat.

A BOOK

OF

POEMS AND
PORTRAITS

BY

DJUNA BARNES

Fragment for 291

2 91 is the attic
     near the Roof.

It is nearer the roof
than any other attic
in the world.

There insomnia
is not a malady—
it is an ideal.

The Dreamer

THE night comes down, in ever-darkening shapes
    that seem—
To grope, with eerie fingers for the window—then—
To rest, to sleep, enfolding me, as in a dream.
      Faith—might I awaken!

And drips the rain with seeming sad, insistent beat.
Shivering across the pane, drooping tear-wise,
And softly patters by, like little fearing feet.
      Faith—'tis weather!

The feathery ash is fluttered; there upon the pane,—
The dying fire casts a flickering ghostly beam,—
Then closes in the night and gently falling rain.
      Faith—what darkness!

Somewhere

SOMEWHERE—I know not where it be—
   A glade lies glad in a dying sun,
A ghost of a tree there dances, too;
But the glade's not me—and the ghost's not you,
Nor the purple slope, nor the woodland dew.
Somewhere—I know not where it be.

Somewhere—I know not where the spot—
Within some leaf-secluded vale,
A grey, low-lying fog drifts by,
Where idle cattle sleeping lie,
But that's not you—nor is it I.
Somewhere—I know not where the spot.

Somewhere—perhaps—who knows—may be—
A lad and a lass could find the way,
Could guide our feet and place your hand
Within mine own in that hidden land,
That you and I might understand.
Somewhere—perhaps—who knows—may be!

Call of the Night

DARK, and the wind-blurred pines,
   With a glimmer of light between.
Then I, entombed for an hourless night
   With the world of things unseen.

Mist, the dust of flowers,
   Leagues, heavy with promise of snow,
And a beckoning road 'twixt vale and hill,
   With the lure that all must know.

A light, my window's gleam,
   Soft, flaring its squares of red—
I lose the ache of the wilderness
   And long for the fire instead.

You too know, old fellow?
   Then, lift up your head and bark.
It's just the call of the lonesome place,
   The winds and the housing dark.

Solitude

I SEEK no solitude but this—
 This one within my little room—
Four candles set apart to watch
 With wistful eyes the coming gloom.

And this, the shrouded mantelpiece
 And sober gap of fireside-place;
And this, the darkened wonder of
 A framed picture of a face.

This is my perfect solitude
 Within my conquering abode,
The goal of haunting memories
 That walk beside a chartless road.

Serenade

THREE paces down the shore, low sounds the lute,
   The better that my longing you may know;
I'm not asking you to come,
         But—can't you go?

Three words, "I love you," and the whole is said—
The greatness of it throbs from sun to sun;
I'm not asking you to walk,
         But—can't you run?

Three paces in the moonlight's glow I stand,
And here within the twilight beats my heart.
I'm not asking you to finish,
         But—to start.

Harvest Time

WHY couldn't we have known
    When love was sweet,
When the world and I lay dreaming
At your feet,
That all the barren things would blossom
In the wheat?

Why couldn't we have known
No bitter gloom
Or any troubled sense or knowledge
Of the tomb.
Could be a master-work when poppies lean,
Bleeding into bloom?

Why couldn't we have known
In younger years—
When life and love were lived
Undimmed by tears—
That no cry of youth or age is wider
Than the ears?

DJUNA BARNES   By Herself

This Much & More

IF my lover were a comet
    Hung in air,
I would braid my leaping body
   In his hair.

Yea, if they buried him ten leagues
   Beneath the loam,
My fingers they would learn to dig
   And I'd plunge home!

A Last Toast

MY tears are falling one by one
 Upon the silence of this bed;
Like rain they crown his quiet head
Like moons they slip within his hair;
They came like wine and passed like prayer
Into the goblets of the dead.

Birth

FORE-loved, fore-crowned, and fore-betrayed,
    And thrice our quality been weighed,
   And thrice our hearts been spit with steel
   To prove us worthier to feel
Both love and hate creep through that blade,
    The wings of doom press tip to tip,
And all dead hands like bricks are laid
    And reach like mansions to the sky—
    The parting, weeping lip to lip,
   That all things born must always die.
And that the seed of Nothing lies
   Yet here within this envied Much—
   So we are forecast, and of such
The child's first sobbing prophesies.

Shadows

A LITTLE trellis stood beside my head,
    And all the tiny fruitage of its vine
Fashioned a shadowy cover to my bed,
And I was madly drunk on shadow wine!

A lily bell hung sidewise, leaning down,
And gowned me in a robe so light and long;
And so I dreamed, and drank, and slept,
    and heard
The lily's song.

Lo, for a house, the shadow of the moon;
For golden money, all the daisy rings;
And for my love, the meadow at my side—
Thus tramps are kings!

The Yellow Jar

WHITE butterflies are creeping near
    This yellow jar where rose-leaves lie,
Like simple nuns in gowns of fear,
Like humor and like tragedy.

And down they steal with throbbing wing
Across the pool of shadows, where
That other bowl of dust is king
With blossoms past, with tear, with prayer.

One was the rose you brought, and one
Was you. The symbol lied—it seemed
You were the summit of the sun;
Now you are less than that you dreamed.

In life we loved you, and in death
There is devotion for you, too;
Only the witless human breath
Is mourning for the death in you.

Yet what of you, I wonder, stands
Without the stillness of the room,
Beyond the reach of rising hands,
Still smiling at this china tomb!

White butterflies are creeping past
The jar of death, the yellow jar;
For butterflies are not the last
To sense things are not as they are!

Antique

A LADY in a cowl of lawn,
　　With straight bound tabs and muted eyes,
And lips fair thin and deftly drawn
　And oddly wise.

A cameo, a ruff of lace,
　A neck cut square, with corners laid,
A thin Greek nose, and near the face
　A polished braid.

Low, sideways looped, of amber stain,
　The pale ears caught within its snare.
A profile like a dagger lain
　Between the hair.

The Lament of Women

A h   M y   G o d !

AH my God, what is it that we love!
   This flesh laid on us like a wrinkled glove?
Bones caught in haste from out some lustful bed,
And for momentum, this a devil's shove.

What is it that hurriedly we kiss,
This mouth that seeks our own, or still more this
Small sorry eye within the cheated head,
As if it mourned the something that we miss.

This pale, this over eager listening ear
The wretched mouth its soft lament to hear,—
To mark the noiseless and the anguished fall
Of still one other warm misshapen tear.

Short arms, and bruised feet long set apart
To walk with us forever from the start.
Ah God, is this the reason that we love—
Because such things are death blows to the heart?

To — — — — — — —

ANOTHER'S veins are set within my days
    His misery, as much as yours, is mine
Yet tell me, is this not a virgin's gaze
    Held fast in thine?

I turn always and blow the candle's flame
Into the darkness, dropping down my tears,
Striking out the ending of the game
    By forty years.

And in the darkness hear the frightened moan
Of him half wounded, unidentified
Some one unutterably alone
    And mystified.

Nay touch me not too tenderly or well
For I have words to every man's distress
And some forgotten ailing hand in hell
    First tore this dress.

Always, yea always, always thus with me
Another's dust shall mix here, when I cease
While yours, my love, a thousand years shall be
    Clotted with peace.

Lines to a Lady

L AY her under the rusty grass,
     With her two eyes heavy and blind
          and done;
Her two hands crossed beneath her breast
     One on one.

Lay her out in the paling eve,
With its sudden tears and white birch-trees;
And let her passing seem to be
     One with these.

Close her out of this hour of grief,
And casting the earth on her, like a breath,
Sew her tenderly, that she may
     Reap her death!

And close her eyes, close, close her lips,
For still, too still is her smitten tongue;
Her hour's over, her breath has passed,
    And her song is sung.

Lay her under the wild red grass
In the fields death-tossed and bowed with rain;
And let her silence seem to move
    Within the grain.

To a Bird

Up from some leafy cover hot with June
     And odorous with spicy mysteries
  Of herbs unknown, a red bird dipping flies,
Whistling a little sadly, out of tune,
     Under a slow moon.

Lifts and turns, and, like blots on a wall,
    Leaves fleeting shadows in its drowsy flight;
    The earth beneath, and all above the night,
And stealing out between the last leaf's fall
        A new bird's call.

Singing its way into the South once more,
    No more returning; and the dropping leaves
    The branches strip like arms thrust
        out of sleeves—
And though the wind doth through the
        whole world roar
    A feather only stirs upon its floor.

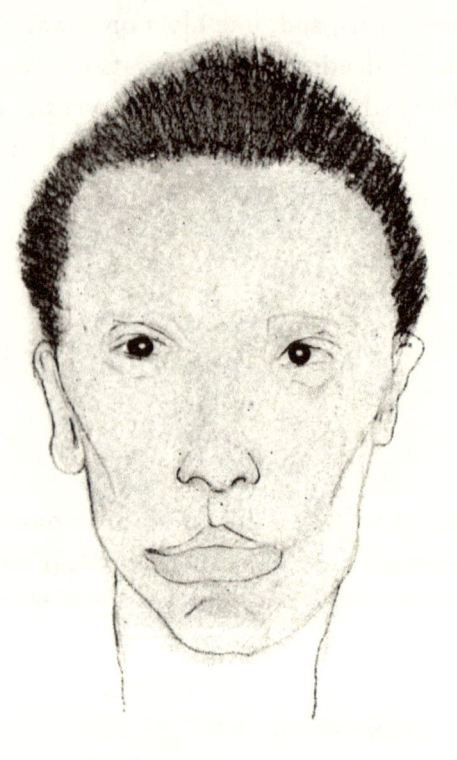

Hush Before Love

A VOICE rose in the darkness, saying "Love,"
   And in the stall the scattered
      mice grew still,
Where yet the white ox slept, and on the sill
The crowing cock paused, and the grey house dove
Turned twice about upon the ledge above.

Paradise

THIS night I've been one hour in Paradise;
   There found a feather from
      the Cock that Crew—
There heard the echo of the Kiss that Slew,
And in the dark, about past agonies
      Hummed little flies.

Pastoral

A FROG leaps out across the lawn,
  And crouches there—all heavy and alone,
And like a blossom, pale and over-blown,
Once more the moon turns dim against the dawn.

Crawling across the straggling panoply
Of little roses, only half in bloom,
It strides within that beamed and lofty room
Where an ebon stallion looms upon the hay.

The stillness moves, and seems to grow immense,
A shudd'ring dog starts, dragging at its chain,
Thin, dusty rats slink down within the grain,
And in the vale the first far bells commence.

Here in the dawn, with mournful doomèd eyes
A cow uprises, moving out to bear
A soft-lipped calf with swarthy birth-swirled hair,
And wide wet mouth, and droll uncertainties.

The grey fowls fight for places in the sun,
The mushrooms flare, and pass like painted fans:
All the world is patient in its plans—
The seasons move forever, one on one.

Small birds lie sprawling vaguely in the heat,
And wanly pluck at shadows on their breasts,
And where the heavy grape-vine leans and rests,
White butterflies lift up their furry feet.

The wheat grows querulous with unseen cats;
A fox strides out in anger through the corn,
Bidding each acre wake and rise to mourn
Beneath its sharps and through its throaty flats.

And so it is, and will be year on year,
Time in and out of date, and still on time
A billion grapes plunge bleeding into wine
And bursting, fall like music on the ear.

The snail that marks the girth of night with slime,
The lonely adder hissing in the fern,
The lizard with its ochre eyes aburn—
Each is before, and each behind its time.

Song in Autumn

THE wind comes down before the creeping night
   And you, my love, are hid within the green
Long grasses; and the dusk steals up between
Each leaf, as through the shadow quick with fright
The startled hare leaps up and out of sight.

The hedges whisper in their loaded boughs
Where warm birds slumber, pressing wing to wing,
All pulsing faintly, like a muted string
Above us where we weary of our vows—
And hidden underground the soft moles drowse.

Lullaby

WHEN I was a young child I slept with a dog,
    I lived without trouble and I thought no harm;
I ran with the boys and I played leap-frog;
Now it is a girl's head that lies on my arm.

Then I grew a little, picked plantain in the yard;
Now I dwell in Greenwich, and the people do not call;
Then I planted pepper-seed and stamped on them hard.
Now I am very quiet and I hardly plan at all.

Then I pricked my finger on a thorn, or a thistle,
Put the finger in my mouth, and ran to my mother.
Now I lie here, with my eyes on a pistol.
There will be a morrow, and another, and another.

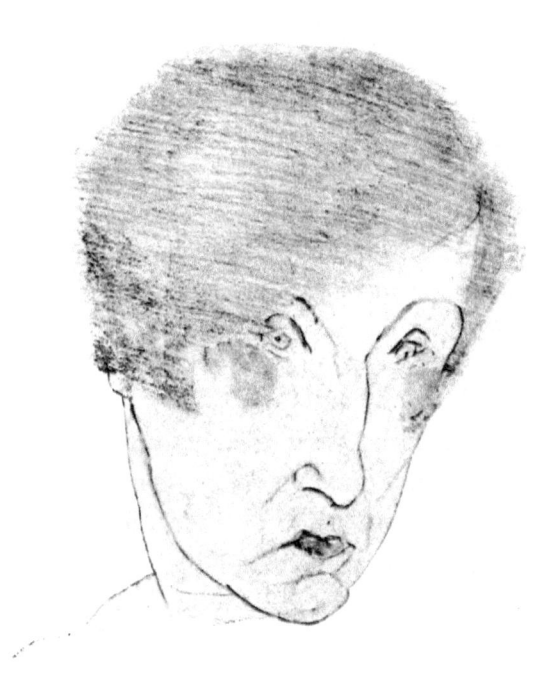

I'd Have You Think of Me

As one who, leaning on the wall, once drew
Thick blossoms down, and hearkened to the hum
Of heavy bees slow rounding the wet plum,
And heard across the fields the patient coo
Of restless birds bewildered with the dew.

As one whose thoughts were mad in painful May,
With melancholy eyes turned toward her love,
And toward the troubled earth whereunder throve
The chilly rye and coming hawthorn spray—
With one lean, pacing hound, for company.

The Flowering Corpse

So still she lies in this closed place apart,
Her feet grown fragile for the ghostly tryst;
Her pulse no longer striking in her wrist,
Nor does its echo wander through her heart.

Over the body and the quiet head
Like stately ferns above an austere tomb,
Soft hairs blow; and beneath her armpits bloom
The drowsy passion flowers of the dead.

First Communion

THE mortal fruit upon the bough
    Hangs above the nuptial bed.
The cat-bird in the tree returns
The forfeit of his mutual vow.

The hard, untimely apple of
The branch that feeds on watered rain
Takes the place upon her lips
Of her late lamented love.

Many hands together press
Shaped within a static prayer
Recall to one the chorister
Docile in his sexless dress.

The temperate winds reclaim the iced
Remorseless vapours of the snow.
The only pattern in the mind
Is the cross behind the Christ.

Finis

FOR you, for me?
  Why then the striking hour,
The wind among the curtains, and the tread
Of some late gardener pulling at the flower
They'll lay between our hearts when we are dead.

FINALE...

Djuna Barnes

FINALE

The Little Review (1918)

In the centre of the room lay the corpse.

The proper number of candles burned at head and feet.

The body had been duly attended to. The undertaker had pared the nails, put the tongue back in the mouth, shut the eyes, and with a cloth dusted with bismuth had touched the edges of the nostrils.

It had been washed and dressed and made to assume the conventional death pose—the hands crossed palm over knuckles. Everything else in the room seemed willing to go on changing—being. He alone remained cold and unwilling, like a stoppage in the atmosphere.

His wife, his mother, and his children knelt about him. His wife cried heavily, resting the middle of her breasts on the hard side of the coffin boards. His mother wept also, but with that comfort of one who has seen both the beginning and the end; with that touch of restfulness that comes to those who like the round, the complete, the final.

His children knelt and did not weep. The little girl's closed palms were damp, and she wanted to look at them but dared not. The boy had that very morning discovered the pleasure of rubbing his head under his nurse's arm when she said "Come, put your shirt on," and he wanted to smile about this, but his eyes refused to grow damp, he could not permit himself the satisfaction.

On the floor, in a corner, lay what had been the dead man's dearest possession—a bright blue scarf embroidered with spots of gold. It had been given to him when passing through Italy, by a long legged Sicilian whom he had loved as one loves who must catch a train.

It was a lovely thing, but much treasuring had lined it; and the marks of his thumbs as they passed over it in pleasant satisfaction had left their tarnish on the little spots of gold.

The shadows grew and darkness fell. The room was silent save for that melancholy murmur of lips that taste tears.

A large rat put his head out of a hole, long dusty, and peered into the room.

The children were going to rise and go to bed soon. The bodies of the mourners had that half-sorrowful, half-bored look of people who do something that hurts too long.

Presently the rat took hold of the scarf and trotted away with it into the darkness of the beyond.

One thing only had the undertaker forgotten to do; he had failed to remove the cotton from the ears of the dead man, who had suffered from ear-ache.

Djuna Barnes, by Terry

A BOOK
By DJUNA BARNES

That almost mythi-
cal personality that
has loomed so large-
ly and intangibly
over modern art in
America — D j u n a
B a r n e s—has here
made itself manifest
in a book as indi-
vidual as its creator.
$2.00.

```
┌─────────────────────────────────┐
│                                 │
│      *This Space for Your*      │
│          *Thoughts*             │
│                                 │
│                                 │
└─────────────────────────────────┘
```

THE OLD EXPRESSIONS ARE WITH US ALWAYS
AND THERE ARE ALWAYS OTHERS

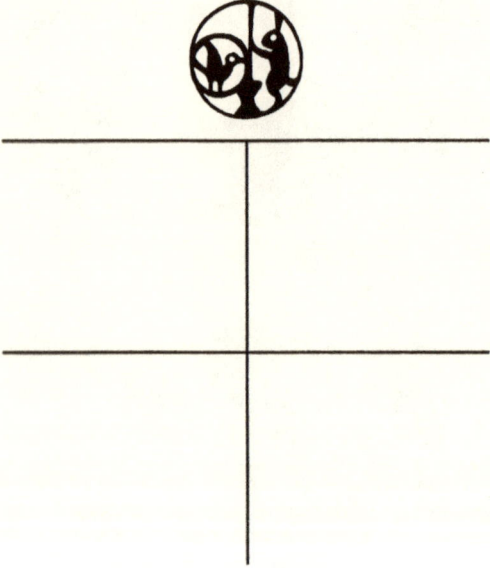

Please handle with care.